D0205609

WHITE DEATH

Heroin kills. But before it kills, heroin changes people. It changes your friend into your enemy; it changes someone you love into a stranger. Heroin kills the body – but first it kills the heart.

Anna Harland thinks that she knows her daughter, Sarah. She knows that Sarah does not sell heroin. But love can change people, too. And Sarah is in love – with a stranger. Why did she have heroin in her bag? Was she carrying it for her boyfriend?

Someone is going to die – but who? The person who uses the heroin? The person who sells it? Or a young girl who never touches it? Heroin is the White Death. And, if it can, the White Death is going to kill them all.

CALGARY PUBLIC LIBRARY

MAY   2017

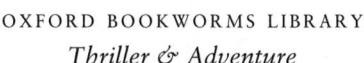

OXFORD BOOKWORMS LIBRARY
Thriller & Adventure

White Death

Stage 1 (400 headwords)

Series Editor: Jennifer Bassett
Founder Editor: Tricia Hedge
Activities Editors: Jennifer Bassett and Alison Baxter

TIM VICARY

White Death

OXFORD UNIVERSITY PRESS

OXFORD
UNIVERSITY PRESS

Great Clarendon Street, Oxford OX2 6DP

Oxford University Press is a department of the University of Oxford.
It furthers the University's objective of excellence in research, scholarship,
and education by publishing worldwide in

Oxford New York

Auckland Cape Town Dar es Salaam Hong Kong Karachi
Kuala Lumpur Madrid Melbourne Mexico City Nairobi
New Delhi Shanghai Taipei Toronto

With offices in

Argentina Austria Brazil Chile Czech Republic France Greece
Guatemala Hungary Italy Japan Poland Portugal Singapore
South Korea Switzerland Thailand Turkey Ukraine Vietnam

OXFORD and OXFORD ENGLISH are registered trade marks of
Oxford University Press in the UK and in certain other countries

This edition © Oxford University Press 2008

The moral rights of the author have been asserted

Database right Oxford University Press (maker)

First published in Oxford Bookworms 1989

13 15 17 19 20 18 16 14

No unauthorized photocopying

All rights reserved. No part of this publication may be reproduced,
stored in a retrieval system, or transmitted, in any form or by any means,
without the prior permission in writing of Oxford University Press,
or as expressly permitted by law, or under terms agreed with the appropriate
reprographics rights organization. Enquiries concerning reproduction
outside the scope of the above should be sent to the ELT Rights Department,
Oxford University Press, at the address above

You must not circulate this book in any other binding or cover
and you must impose this same condition on any acquirer

Any websites referred to in this publication are in the public domain and
their addresses are provided by Oxford University Press for information only.
Oxford University Press disclaims any responsibility for the content

ISBN 978 0 19 478923 3

A complete recording of this Bookworms edition of
White Death is available in an audio pack ISBN 978 0 19 478891 5

Printed in China

ACKNOWLEDGEMENTS
Illustrated by: Maya Gavin

Word count (main text): 6,600 words

For more information on the Oxford Bookworms Library,
visit www.oup.com/elt/gradedreaders

CONTENTS

Chapter 1

The woman stood in front of the prison. The prison was a big, dirty building in the biggest town of a hot country. The woman was very hot, and she did not like the noise from all the cars in the road. She was an Englishwoman and she did not like hot countries or a lot of noise. She was tall, about fifty years old, with blue eyes and a long face. Her face was red, and she looked tired and angry.

She knocked at the door of the prison. For a long time nothing happened. Then a little window opened in the door, and a man looked out at her.

Anna Harland knocked at the door of the prison.

'Yes? What do you want?'

'I want to see my daughter. It's very important.'

'Name?'

'Anna Harland.'

'Is that your name or your daughter's name?'

'It's my name. My daughter's name is Sarah Harland.'

'You can't visit her today. Come back on Wednesday.'

'No! I came from England to see her today. It's very important. She's going to court tomorrow. Please take me to her – now!'

'Wait a minute.'

The little window closed, but the door did not open. The woman waited in front of the door for a long time. A lot of people in the road looked at her. One or two young men laughed, but she did not move. She stood there in the hot road in front of the prison door, and waited.

After twenty minutes, the door opened. 'Come with me,' the man said. The woman went in with him. It was dark in the prison, and at first she could not see very well. She walked for a long time, past hundreds of doors. Then the man opened one of them.

'In here,' he said. 'You can have ten minutes.'

Anna Harland walked into the room and the man went in after her. He closed the door behind him. There was a table in the room, and two chairs. On one of the chairs sat her daughter, Sarah. She was a tall girl, about nineteen years old, with big blue eyes.

'Sarah!' Anna said, and put out her arms.

'Mother!' she said. 'I'm very happy to see you.' And she got up and began to run across the room to her mother.

'Sarah!' Anna said, and put out her arms. But the man moved quickly and stood between them.

'No,' he said to Anna. 'I'm sorry. I know you're her mother. You can talk, but that's all. Please sit down at the table. I am here to watch you.'

The mother and daughter sat down at the table. Anna's hands were near Sarah's on the table. She looked carefully at her daughter. Sarah's dress and face were dirty. 'She's tired, and unhappy,' Anna thought.

'Sarah, what happened?' she said. 'We have ten minutes to talk. No more. Tell me, please, quickly. I want to help you.'

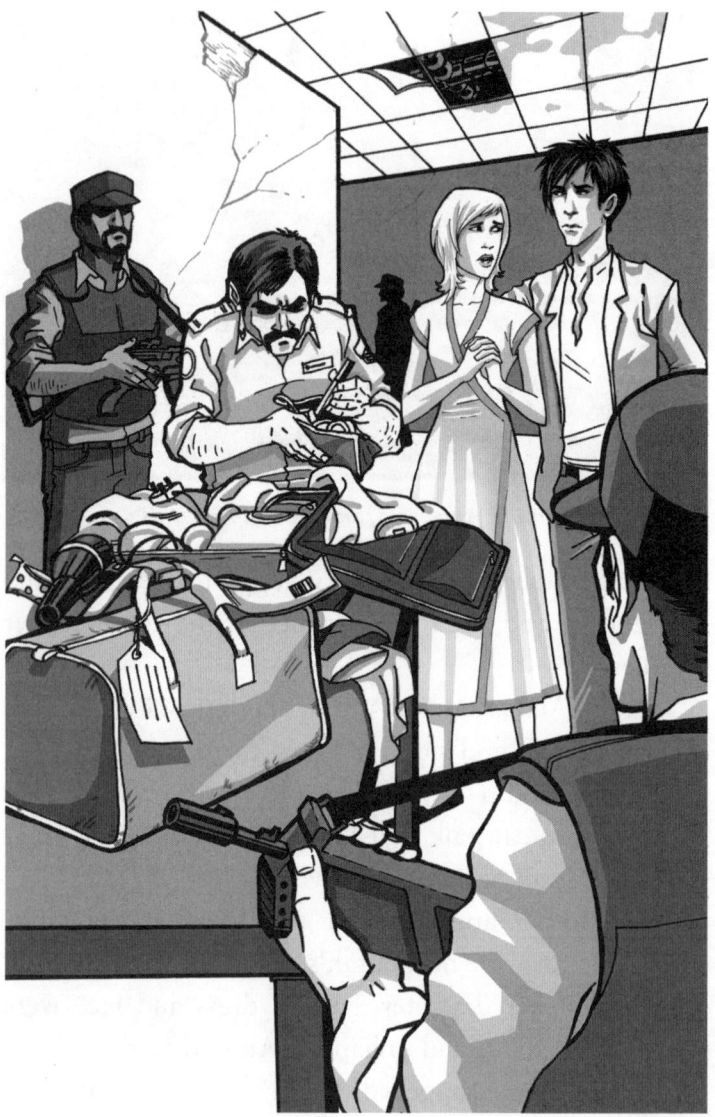

'At the airport, when we arrived ... The police stopped us,
and looked in our bags.'

Sarah looked at her mother. 'Oh, mother, I'm happy you're here. I wanted you to come. Mother, I . . . I didn't do it. It isn't true. Please believe me.'

'Of course I believe you, Sarah. But tell me about it. What happened? Quickly. Begin at the beginning.'

'Yes, but . . . I don't know . . . When did it begin? I don't know . . . I don't understand it.'

'Why did the police arrest you? When did they bring you to this prison?'

'Last week, I think. Yes, last week. At the airport, when we arrived . . . The police stopped us, and looked in our bags. Then . . .'

Sarah looked down at the table. 'She's crying,' Anna thought. 'She's very unhappy.'

'What happened then, Sarah?' her mother asked.

'They . . . they said there were drugs in my bag. Then they took me into a room and told me to take my dress off. They looked for more drugs, but they found nothing. Then . . . then they brought me here.'

'I see. Where were the drugs, then? Where did they find them?'

'Oh. They didn't tell you?' Sarah stopped crying. She looked up, and there was a smile on her face. But it was not a happy smile. 'The drugs were in a tube of toothpaste. A toothpaste tube with drugs in it . . . heroin . . . not toothpaste.'

'And you didn't know about it?'

'No, mother, of course not. Do you think I clean my teeth with heroin?'

Anna Harland smiled. It was difficult to smile, because she was afraid. But she smiled because she wanted to help her daughter.

'I know you don't clean your teeth with heroin. You have very good teeth, Sarah. But . . . what about Stephen? Did he know about the heroin? Did he put it in the toothpaste tube?'

'Stephen? No . . . why do you ask about Stephen, mother?'

'Well, is he in prison too? You said "us" and "our bags". Did the police arrest him too?'

'Oh . . . no,' Sarah's face was unhappy. 'No. I wasn't with Stephen, mother. You see, Stephen and I . . . well, we aren't friends now. I left him about two months ago . . . and then I met Hassan.'

'Hassan?'

'Yes. I was with Hassan at the airport. Stephen was on the plane too – I don't know why – but he wasn't with me. It's Hassan – he was with me. Hassan's important to me now, not Stephen.'

Anna looked at her daughter. 'I see. And did the police arrest this Hassan too? Is he in prison?'

'Yes, he is. They arrested him but I can't see him. I asked them. I wanted to see him. But they said "no". Mother, I'm sure Hassan didn't know about the heroin. He's a good man . . . he didn't know, I'm sure.'

Stephen was on the plane too.

'Then why was the heroin in your bag, Sarah?'

'I don't know, mother . . . I don't know.'

The man looked at the clock in the room. 'I'm sorry, Mrs Harland,' he said. 'But that's ten minutes. It's time to go.'

Anna Harland stood up slowly. 'All right,' she said. 'But don't be afraid, Sarah. I'm coming to the court tomorrow.'

'Yes, mother,' Sarah said. 'Thank you. The police are bringing Hassan to court tomorrow too, I think. You can see him there. He's a good man, mother, and . . . I'm sure he didn't know about the drugs.'

'Perhaps,' Anna said. She walked slowly to the door, and then stood by the door and looked at her daughter

again. 'Sarah . . . you are telling me the truth, aren't
you?'

Sarah began to cry again. 'Yes, mother, of course I
am. I always tell you the truth, you know that.'

Anna smiled. 'Yes, Sarah,' she said quietly. 'Yes, I
believe you.' She went through the door and the man
went out after her.

Sarah sat quietly at the table in the room, and looked
at her hands. 'Yes,' she thought. 'I told you the truth,
mother. I always tell you the truth. But I didn't tell you
everything . . .' She put her head in her hands.

Chapter 2

Anna Harland left the prison and went to talk to the
police. She waited a long time in a small office, but after
an hour a policeman came into the room. He was a big
man, about fifty-five years old, with brown eyes and a
nice smile. He moved very slowly and quietly.

'Good afternoon, Mrs Harland,' he said. 'My name is
Detective Inspector Aziz. I . . . arrested your daughter
three days ago. I'm very sorry for you. This is a very
unhappy thing for a mother . . .'

'It's a very unhappy thing for my daughter, Inspector,'
Anna said angrily. 'Because she didn't do it. She's
innocent, you know. She knows nothing about those
drugs.'

'My name is Inspector Aziz. I arrested your daughter.'

Detective Inspector Aziz looked at her carefully for a minute. He did not know many English women. 'She has an interesting face,' he thought. 'Very blue eyes, and a long nose. She is not afraid of me, and she is not crying. Perhaps she wants to know the truth. Perhaps she can help me, too.'

'Well, Mrs Harland,' he said slowly. 'It's difficult for me. Is your daughter telling the truth? Is she innocent? Because the drugs were in her bag, you know.'

'I know,' Anna said. 'But she was with a young man . . . Hassan. She doesn't know him very well, I think. Tell me about him, please. I want to know.'

Inspector Aziz smiled. 'All right,' he said. 'But first, tell me about your daughter. Why was she on that plane? Why did she come to this country? Tell me.'

Anna Harland looked at him. 'He's a nice man,' she thought. 'He listens to people. Perhaps he wants to help. Perhaps he can understand Sarah.'

'Do you have daughters?' she asked.

'Yes,' the Inspector answered. 'Two.'

'Then perhaps you can understand,' Anna said. 'Sarah is nineteen. She finished school last year, and she worked for six months in a hospital to get some money. Then she and her boyfriend, Stephen, visited a lot of countries. They went to Greece, Turkey, India, Australia – and now they're here. They're young, and they want to see new countries and new towns and new people. That's all.'

'I see,' the Inspector said. 'But sometimes young people do things – bad things – because they are in a different country and they need money.'

'Not Sarah,' Anna said. 'And not heroin. Sarah worked in a hospital, and she knows about heroin. She knows it can kill people. I'm a doctor, and she wants to be a doctor, too.'

'I see,' the Inspector said again. He looked at her, and thought, but he said nothing.

'Now,' Anna said. 'Tell me about this young man, Hassan.'

'All right,' the Inspector said. He took some papers from the table and began to read to her. 'But we don't know very much about him. He's a rich boy, from a good family. His father has two or three shops, I think.

And the police in his town know him, too. Last year his father gave him a new car – a very fast car. And . . . listen to this! One day he hit a police car, and the police car went into the river! What a story! His father bought a new car for the police. His father has a lot of money.'

The Inspector smiled, but Anna looked unhappy. 'Oh dear,' she said. 'That's not very good.'

'No,' he said. 'It isn't good. But this story about the heroin is worse. Much worse. I don't like this story.'

Chapter 3

Next morning, Anna Harland went to the court. She was first there. She sat in the courtroom and waited.

Next morning, Anna Harland went to the court.

Sarah looked across the courtroom and saw her mother.

A lot of people came in, and she saw a man and his wife. 'Perhaps they're Hassan's father and mother,' Anna thought. But she did not want to talk to them.

The lawyers came in next, with a lot of papers. They sat at a table in front of her, and talked quietly.

'Those two lawyers,' Anna thought, 'they're old friends. But one of them wants my daughter to die, and one wants her to be free.'

After the lawyers, the jury came in – twelve people, men and women. They sat down and watched the lawyers. They looked at Anna, and then talked quietly about her. 'These people don't look very important,' she thought. 'But they are the most important people here. They're going to say "she did it" . . . or "she didn't do it". And then Sarah comes home to me . . . or she dies.' She watched their faces carefully.

Then some policemen came in. Inspector Aziz saw Anna and smiled at her. But Anna did not talk to him, because Sarah came in at the same time. She looked afraid, and her face was very white. She looked across the courtroom, saw her mother, and gave her an unhappy smile.

There were two policemen behind Sarah, but Anna did not look at them. She looked at the tall dark young man next to Sarah – Hassan!

'He's about twenty years old,' Anna thought. 'He's very tall. But he has a nice face, and very beautiful dark eyes. Sarah likes him, and I can understand that. But he looks very unhappy, too . . . and afraid. His hands are moving all the time.'

Hassan looked at Sarah and smiled. She smiled back at him. Anna wanted to talk to Sarah, but just then a policeman said loudly: 'All stand, please.' Everybody stood up, and the judge came into the courtroom. He went to his chair and sat down.

The police lawyer began. 'These two young people came into our country last week,' he said. 'The young man lives in this country, and the young woman is English. At the airport, the police looked in their bags, and they found three tubes of toothpaste. These tubes of toothpaste!'

He had the three tubes in his hand, and he looked at them. Everybody could see them.

'But are they tubes of toothpaste?' he asked. 'No, men and women of the jury, they are not. Oh no. There is no toothpaste in these tubes. There is heroin in them! Yes, heroin . . . a bad, dirty drug. Perhaps the worst drug. People die from this drug. The "White Death", they call it.'

The lawyer stopped, and looked at the jury. He waited for a minute or two. The courtroom was very quiet. Then he began again.

'But why, you ask me – why did these two young people have this heroin in their bags? I can tell you. Because heroin is one of the most expensive drugs, too. They can sell these tubes of heroin in our country for

'There is no toothpaste in these tubes. There is heroin in them.'

perhaps eighty thousand pounds. Eighty thousand pounds! Easy money! And, men and women of the jury, many people in our country – young people, school-children, too – take this drug. At first it's exciting and they feel happy. But then they need more and more heroin, and they need more money to buy the drug. They leave their homes and families. They take more heroin . . . and more. They can't stop. Soon the drug begins to kill them. And in the end they die. The "White Death". It's not a quick death, and it's not an easy death. Yes, men and women of the jury, many young people and children – your children and my children, remember! – die because of this drug.'

The lawyer stopped again. The jury watched him, and waited.

'He's very good,' Anna thought. 'Very, very good. He's telling the jury an exciting story, and they like him. But it isn't good for Sarah.'

The lawyer walked across the courtroom and stood in front of the jury. 'But, my friends,' he said to the jury, 'we have a law in this country. And the law is not difficult to understand. When people bring heroin into this country, they bring death, too. We need to stop these people. And how can we do that? The answer is easy. The law for these people is death.'

The lawyer walked back to his table. 'Now please look at these two young people here in this court,' he said to the jury. 'They brought heroin into this country. The airport police are going to tell you about it. Please listen carefully. It's not a long story. And remember . . . the law is death.'

The police lawyer sat down, and an airport policeman went to the front of the courtroom. Anna felt ill. She looked at Sarah. Sarah was white-faced and very afraid. Anna closed her eyes. 'Sarah,' she thought, 'Oh, Sarah.'

The police lawyer stood up again. 'Please tell the court about Sarah Harland and Hassan,' he said to the airport policeman.

'Yes, sir,' said the policeman. 'I found two tubes of toothpaste in the girl's bag, and one tube in the young man's bag. All three tubes had heroin in them.'

'Thank you.' The police lawyer sat down, and Mr Cheng – Sarah's and Hassan's lawyer – stood up.

'What did Sarah Harland say when you found the heroin?' he asked.

'Nothing, sir. She began to cry.'

'I see. Was she afraid?'

The policeman thought for a minute. 'I don't know, sir. Perhaps she was, yes.'

'And she said nothing? Are you sure?'

The policeman thought again. 'Well, yes, sir, I think perhaps she said: "This isn't my toothpaste. This is all wrong."'

'I see. And what about the young man, Hassan? What did he say?'

'Well, sir, he was very angry. He said: "It's not heroin. That's not true! You put it there!"'

'I see. Thank you. Now tell me, why did you look in

'What did you say?' Mr Cheng asked the airport policeman, very angrily.

these two young people's bags? You don't usually look
in everyone's bags. There isn't time.'

The policeman thought again. 'Well, no, sir, we don't.
I . . . I'm afraid I can't tell you, sir.'

'What did you say?' Mr Cheng asked, very angrily.
'Of course you can tell me! This is a court of law!' He
looked at the judge. 'This is a very important question.
We need an answer!'

The judge looked at the airport policeman. 'I'm
sorry,' he said. 'Please answer the question. The court
needs to know the answer.'

'Yes, sir. Well, you see, there was a telephone call.
Someone telephoned me before the plane arrived. The
telephone caller said: "There's some heroin on the
plane. A young man and a young woman are carrying
it."'

'I see,' Mr Cheng said. He smiled. 'That's very
interesting. And who made this telephone call?'

'I don't know,' the policeman said. 'It was a man, and
he talked in English. I don't know his name.'

Suddenly Anna heard a noise. She looked behind her at
the door of the courtroom. A tall young man came into
the back of the room. Anna knew him at once. It was
Stephen, Sarah's old boyfriend. A policeman took him
to a chair near Anna. He saw Anna, and for a second he
looked afraid. But then he smiled, and sat down next to
her.

Stephen, Sarah's old boyfriend, came into the back of the room.

'Mrs Harland!' he said quietly. 'It's good to see you. When did you arrive?'

'Yesterday,' she said. 'Why are you late?'

'I couldn't find the court,' he answered. He looked very unhappy. 'Tell me how to help,' he said. 'I want to help Sarah, but what can I do? I was on the plane too, but I couldn't help her. I don't want her to die!'

'Stay with me, young man,' Anna said quietly. 'We can help her – I'm sure we can!'

Later that morning, Sarah went to the front of the courtroom. Her face was very white, and her eyes were red with crying. Her lawyer – Mr Cheng – began to ask her questions.

'Now, Miss Harland, why did you come to this country?' he asked quietly, and smiled at her.

'Because I like going to different countries. I want to meet new people.'

'And why were you with this young man?'

'Because . . .' Sarah stopped and looked down at her feet. Nobody could see her face. She began again, very quietly, but nobody could hear her.

'I'm sorry. We can't hear you. Can you say that again, please?'

Sarah looked up. She looked quickly at her mother, and then at Hassan.

'Because I love him.'

Anna felt old and tired. She looked at the tall young man with the beautiful dark eyes. 'It was his heroin,' she

'Because I love him,' Sarah said.

thought. 'I'm sure it was. He buys and sells heroin, and he put it in my daughter's bag. And now she says she loves him!'

Stephen sat next to her. He did not move, and he watched Sarah all the time. But she did not look at him.

Mr Cheng waited a minute, and then he questioned Sarah again. 'Did you know about the heroin in those tubes of toothpaste?' he asked.

'No,' Sarah said quickly. 'Of course I didn't!'

'And what about Hassan? Did he know about the heroin? Please think about your answer.'

'No, I'm sure he didn't know. It wasn't our heroin!' Sarah's blue eyes were angry. 'We didn't put the heroin in the toothpaste tubes. We're innocent!'

'Thank you, Miss Harland,' Mr Cheng said quietly, and sat down.

The police lawyer stood up. 'Miss Harland. How much money did you have in your bag?'

'Um . . . about fifty pounds, I think.'

'That's not very much. This is an expensive country, you know. How much can you buy . . . with your fifty pounds?'

Sarah did not have an answer. 'Um . . . I don't know,' she began. 'I usually live very cheaply . . .'

'Did you need more money?' The lawyer's questions came quickly now. 'Of course you needed more money. You wanted to sell that heroin. You wanted to be rich. Is that right?'

'No! No! That's not true!'

The lawyer said nothing for a minute. He looked at the jury, and smiled. Then he said, 'Do you think toothpaste is very expensive in this country, Miss Harland?'

'Er . . . no, I don't think . . . er . . . I don't know.'

'Well, I can tell you, it isn't. Toothpaste is cheap here. So why did you bring three tubes of toothpaste with you? How often do you clean your teeth, Miss Harland? Six times a day? Or seven, or eight, times a day, perhaps?'

Sarah looked very unhappy. 'No . . . I don't know . . . Hassan . . .'

'Yes?' the lawyer said quickly. 'Hassan? Are you going to say "Hassan gave it to me"? You love this young man, but you don't want to die. Nobody wants to die. And now you're going to say "It was Hassan's toothpaste". Is that your answer, Miss Harland?'

'No!' Sarah said angrily. 'Of course not! It was *my* toothpaste. But . . .'

'Thank you, Miss Harland.' The police lawyer sat down. 'I have no more questions.'

Chapter 4

At one o'clock the judge left the court for an hour. Anna Harland talked to Sarah for ten minutes. Sarah cried at first.

'I don't like that police lawyer!' she said. 'Those questions were very difficult. I couldn't answer them.'

'It doesn't matter,' her mother said. 'Your lawyer – Mr Cheng – is very good. And Stephen is here too now. We're all going to help you.'

Sarah was angry. 'Don't talk to me about Stephen!' she said. 'I don't like him. I don't want to see him here!'

'But Sarah – he was your boyfriend for two years! He wants to help you.'

Sarah began to cry again. 'Perhaps he does want to help me. I don't know. But he's different now, mother, you don't understand. His eyes are different. They're . . . I don't know. And he can't sit quietly and talk to people now. His body is moving all the time. He came to see me in our hotel the night before we came to this country, and . . . I didn't like him, mother! Why is he here? He doesn't love me now, and I don't love him!'

Anna listened carefully to her daughter, and then she went to see Mr Cheng and Inspector Aziz. Stephen went with her.

'Who made that phone call to the police at the airport?
We need to know that.'

'Who made that phone call to the police at the airport?' she asked. 'We need to know that!'

'Yes,' Mr Cheng said. 'That's very important. Can the police tell us?'

'Perhaps,' the Inspector said. 'But it's very difficult. It was not a long telephone call. And the man didn't give his name. Perhaps he was a policeman, and he knew about the heroin.'

'Perhaps,' Mr Cheng said. 'But then, perhaps he put the heroin there. And he wanted the police to find it. Perhaps someone doesn't like your daughter, Mrs Harland?'

'I don't know,' Anna said slowly. 'But perhaps . . .'

But then the judge came back into the courtroom, and everybody stopped talking.

The judge then called Hassan. Hassan stood up and

went to the front of the courtroom. 'He's a rich boy,' Anna thought. 'That shirt and those shoes are very expensive.'

Hassan stood there, tall and very quiet. He waited for the questions. He did not look afraid. But when Mr Cheng looked at his papers and asked the first question, Hassan closed his eyes.

'Did you know about the heroin in those tubes of toothpaste?'

'No, sir.'

'Did Sarah know?'

'No, sir.'

'Who bought the toothpaste?'

Hassan closed his eyes again for two or three seconds. Then he answered, 'I did, sir.'

'You did? You're sure of that?'

'Yes, sir. I'm sure. I clean my teeth a lot, you see.' Hassan smiled for a moment.

'Well, he does have very white teeth,' Anna thought.

'Sarah . . .' Hassan began. Then he stopped.

'Yes?'

Again Hassan closed his eyes and waited for a second. Then he looked at the jury, and said very loudly: 'Sarah did not buy the toothpaste. I bought it. I bought all three tubes of toothpaste. It was *my* toothpaste.'

Anna sat up in her chair and looked carefully at Hassan. 'That's interesting,' she thought. 'Perhaps he does love Sarah!'

'I see,' Mr Cheng said. 'And when did you first meet Sarah Harland?'

'About two months ago. I was in Australia. We were in the same hotel. She had a . . . a difficult time with her boyfriend and I helped her.'

Anna looked at Stephen. He was very angry, and he hit the chair in front of him with his hand.

'I see,' Mr Cheng said again. Then he asked his next question. 'Do you usually carry a lot of money? How much money did you have at the airport?'

'About eighty pounds, I think. That's OK. When I need more money, I get some work for a week or two. We don't need much money.'

'And do you sometimes take heroin?'

'No, sir. Never.'

'Thank you. Stay there, please.'

Mr Cheng sat down and the police lawyer stood up. He smiled at Hassan, but it was not a nice smile.

'Now, Hassan. You bought the toothpaste, but it was in Miss Harland's bag. Why? Why did she carry it for you? Or do you always ask your women to carry things for you?' He smiled.

Hassan said nothing. The lawyer began again. 'You had eighty pounds, you say. But eighty thousand pounds is better than eighty pounds, I think. What do *you* think?'

'Of course it is. But I don't sell heroin. It's wrong to sell heroin.'

*Stephen was very angry and he hit the chair
in front of him with his hand.*

The lawyer moved his papers on the table. He looked at the jury. 'So you are a very good young man with very clean teeth but no money. You met a young English girl. She was unhappy with her boyfriend, so you helped her and took her away with you. Is that right? Oh dear! It's not a very good story, you know. I don't believe it, and I don't think the jury believes it, young man.'

He stopped for a minute. Then he looked at Hassan, and said loudly: 'You don't love Sarah Harland, and she doesn't love you. You went with her because she could help you. And she went with you because she wanted the money. She carried the heroin for you to sell. That's right, isn't it? You put the heroin in the toothpaste tubes, and she knew about it. Is that the true story, young man? I think it is.'

'No! I ...' Hassan began angrily. But the lawyer did not listen.

'No! I . . .' Hassan began angrily. But the lawyer did not listen. He sat down.

'I have no more questions,' he said to the judge.

Chapter 5

The judge looked at his papers and then at the jury. 'It is now four o'clock in the afternoon,' he said. 'We can begin again in the morning. Please be here at ten o'clock.'

The judge stood up and left the courtroom. The jury left too, and the police took Sarah and Hassan back to the prison.

Anna looked at Stephen. 'Well, young man,' she said. 'What can we do now? We have sixteen hours before tomorrow morning.'

'I don't know,' Stephen said. He looked at her for a minute, then he looked away, over her head, at the front of the court. 'I'm sure Hassan knew about the heroin,' he said. 'He put it in her bag, I'm sure he did. Sarah is innocent. But he isn't.'

Mr Cheng came and stood with them.

'She's innocent,' Stephen said again. 'But Hassan's going to die.'

Mr Cheng looked at Stephen carefully. 'Perhaps,' he said slowly. 'But did you listen to Hassan in court? He said: "Sarah did not buy the toothpaste. It was *my*

'She's innocent,' Stephen said. 'But Hassan's going to die.'

toothpaste." Now why did he say that? It was not an easy thing to say, you know. What is the jury going to think about it?'

'It doesn't matter,' Stephen said angrily. 'Because it wasn't toothpaste, and he didn't buy it in a shop! He made those tubes, because he wanted to sell the heroin. And he's going to die. That's the law in this country.'

Anna looked at Stephen and said nothing. 'He's very angry,' she thought. 'His face is red and he's talking very quickly. Does he want to kill Hassan? And what's the matter with his eyes?'

Mr Cheng watched Stephen too. 'But who made that telephone call? It's important and I want to know,' he said. 'I'm going to ask the police now. Would you like to come with me, Mrs Harland?'

'Yes, of course,' Anna said. 'Stephen, are you coming?'

'Yes . . . er, no, no,' Stephen said. 'I'm going to meet a man. I think he can help us.'

'All right,' Anna said. 'But when can I meet you? I need to talk to you, about Hassan. Can I come to your hotel tonight?'

'Er, no, not tonight,' Stephen said quickly. His face was now white, and he looked tired and ill. His hands and body moved all the time. 'Come to my hotel tomorrow morning. Bye!' He walked quickly out of the courtroom.

Anna and Mr Cheng watched him. Inspector Aziz was near the door, and he watched Stephen, too.

Chapter 6

Anna and Mr Cheng talked to the police, but the police could tell them nothing more about the telephone call to the airport. Inspector Aziz telephoned two or three people, and then he talked to Anna again. When Anna left Inspector Aziz, she was much happier.

Then she went to the prison to see Sarah. The man took her to Sarah's room. Anna and Sarah sat at the table, and the man stood and watched.

'It was a bad day, mother. I'm sorry,' Sarah said slowly. Her eyes were not red now, but she looked very tired. Her hands were near her mother's, on the table.

'It wasn't a very good day, that's true,' Anna said. 'But you have a very good lawyer, you know. The jury likes him.'

'But it doesn't help,' Sarah said. 'There was heroin in the toothpaste tubes, and the tubes were in my bag. What can Mr Cheng do? The heroin was in my bag, mother! The jury knows that!'

Anna looked at her daughter carefully. 'Perhaps Hassan put it there, Sarah,' she said. 'You like him, I know, and he looks nice, but . . .'

'Mother, I love him! I said that in court. You heard me. And Hassan loves me, too! And he does *not* buy or sell heroin! I . . .' Sarah stopped talking, and put her hands on her stomach.

'What's the matter?' Anna asked. She looked at the man. 'Quickly – she's ill. Get a doctor!'

The man ran from the room, and Anna put her arms round her daughter. She waited, and then Sarah sat up.

'It's all right, mother,' she said. Her face was very white, but she looked a little better. 'It happens sometimes. I often feel ill, and I don't like to eat much. But it's not very bad. I think I'm going to stay alive because of it.' She gave her mother a smile.

'What? What are you saying? What are you talking about?' Anna cried.

'My baby.' Sarah's face looked different now – half smiling, half afraid. 'Mother, don't be angry, please. I'm

'Mother, don't be angry, please. I'm going to have
Hassan's baby.'

going to have a baby. It's Hassan's baby. I . . . we
wanted to come to England, and tell you about it there,
but now we can't. I love him, and he wants to be my
husband, mother. Mother? Please don't be angry.'

Anna's face was white now. For nearly a minute she
could say nothing. She wanted to cry, but she didn't. At
last she said, 'Oh, Sarah! What's going to happen to this
baby?'

Sarah looked at her hands. 'Nothing, mother. I asked
Mr Cheng about that. They can't kill me, you see,
because I'm going to have a baby. They can't kill a
mother *and* her baby. That's the law. But . . . that
doesn't help Hassan.'

Anna heard a noise and looked at the door. 'Listen,
Sarah,' she said quickly. 'Before the doctor comes . . .

I'm not angry, and I do love you, Sarah, of course. But listen. I talked to Inspector Aziz again today. I think he can help you – and Hassan too. So don't be afraid, please. And . . .'

The door opened, and the man came in with a woman doctor. Anna stood up. She took Sarah's hand.

'I'm going now, Sarah. But don't be afraid. You're going to be all right – I'm sure of it!'

Chapter 7

Next morning, at half past four, Anna Harland stood in a quiet road in front of a hotel. She waited, and then she

Next morning, at half past four, Anna stood in a quiet road in front of a hotel.

heard a car behind the hotel. The car doors opened and closed. She waited quietly, and then looked down the road. A man walked into the road and stood next to a shop. He did not look at Anna. But Anna looked at him, and smiled. Then she walked into the hotel.

She went upstairs and knocked on the door of a bedroom. A man answered.

'Who is it?'

'It's me, Stephen,' she said. 'Anna Harland. Open the door, please. I want to talk to you.'

The door opened, and Stephen looked out slowly. 'Anna? What are you doing here at this time? It's . . .'

Anna walked quickly into the room. 'Yes. It's half past four. Sarah is in court again at ten o'clock. I need your help, young man. Please get up.'

'But . . . what can I do?'

Anna looked at him. 'You went to see a man last night. What happened? Can he help Sarah?'

Stephen answered slowly. He did not look at Anna. 'No. I'm sorry. He can't.'

Anna was cold and angry. 'I see,' she said. 'Well, can you and I help her then? Tell me, Stephen, what do you know about Hassan?'

'Hassan?' Stephen said angrily. 'Well, we met him in Australia, and Sarah went away with him. She doesn't understand him, but I do – he's a rich young man with a beautiful body. He likes playing with girls, but he doesn't love her!'

'And do you love her, Stephen?'

Stephen did not answer at once. For two or three seconds Anna waited. 'He doesn't know,' she thought. 'He can't answer the question.'

'Yes, Mrs Harland. Of course I love her.'

'But he's not looking at me,' Anna thought. 'He's looking out of the window. He's not thinking about Sarah.'

'Stephen,' Anna asked quietly, 'did you go to see Sarah and Hassan in Australia, the night before they came to this country?'

Stephen looked up at her. 'Er . . . yes, I went to their hotel,' he said. 'I asked Sarah to leave Hassan and come back to me. But how did you know that?'

'Sarah told me, of course. Was Hassan there?'

'No. He . . .' Stephen stopped. Then he said, 'Why do you ask?'

Anna opened her handbag. 'Look at this,' she said. 'What is it? Do you know?'

He looked at it, and then at Anna. 'A tube of toothpaste. Why?'

'That's right. A policeman gave it to me. And he took it from a man. You met that man last night, Stephen. You gave him ten tubes of toothpaste. What was in those tubes of toothpaste, Stephen?'

Stephen said nothing. He looked at the toothpaste, and stood up. But Anna was between him and the door. She gave the toothpaste to him.

'Would you like to clean your teeth, Stephen?'

He began to move to the door, but Anna took his arm. 'You don't love Sarah, do you, Stephen? You hate her, because she left you! You put three of these tubes in Sarah's bag, and then you phoned the police. You told them about the tubes in my daughter's bag . . . You want Sarah to die!'

'No!' Stephen said. 'No, no . . . not Sarah . . . Hassan! I put them in Hassan's bag, not Sarah's. I wanted Hassan to die!'

He opened the door quickly, and then stopped. A man stood there – Inspector Aziz. He put his hand on Stephen's arm.

'It's an old story, young man,' he said. 'It happens

Stephen began to move towards the door.

every day. My first girlfriend left me for a new man. I was very angry too. I hated him. But I didn't want to kill him. Come on. Let's go. You can tell your story to the judge.'

Chapter 8

At eleven o'clock that morning, Sarah and Hassan were free. Sarah stood with her mother, Inspector Aziz, and Mr Cheng. She smiled happily.

'Mother, you're wonderful! Now I can be happy! But . . . how did you know about Stephen?'

Inspector Aziz answered. 'Young woman,' he said. 'Remember, your mother is a doctor. She knew Stephen was ill because of his eyes, and his body. His eyes are very big and dark, and his body is always moving . . .'

'Well, yes,' Anna said. 'But you helped me, Sarah. You said he was different – remember? And I looked at him carefully, and began to think. Heroin does that to people.'

'He did a very bad thing,' Sarah said slowly, 'but I feel sorry for him now. When is he going to court, Inspector?'

'I don't know,' the Inspector said. 'In two weeks, perhaps. But don't think about him. Would you like to see our beautiful country, Mrs Harland? Where would you like to go?'

'Mother you're wonderful! But ... how did you know about
Stephen?' asked Sarah.

Anna smiled at him. 'Thank you. But I can't stay. Tomorrow, I'm going back to England, to talk to Stephen's mother and father.'

Inspector Aziz looked at her, and said nothing for a minute. Then he said quietly: 'Yes. I feel very sorry for them. It kills a lot of young people, this heroin.'

'Yes. But it isn't going to kill my daughter. She isn't going to die now.' Anna took Sarah's hand. 'So thank you again, Inspector Aziz and Mr Cheng. And goodbye. Now I'm going to have a long cold drink in a quiet garden with my daughter and her new young man. I want to know a lot more about him.'

Hassan stood with his mother and father near the door of the court. Anna Harland put her hand on her daughter's arm, and smiled at them.

GLOSSARY

arrest to take bad people to prison

baby a very young child

believe to think that something or someone is true or right

buy (past tense **bought**) to get something with money

clean *(adj)* not dirty

clean *(v)* to make something clean

court *(n)* a place where people (judges, lawyers, a jury) listen to law cases

death when a life finishes

drug aspirin is a good drug; heroin is a bad drug

hate opposite of 'to love'

heroin a very bad drug (usually white); when people take heroin, at first they feel good, but then they cannot stop taking it (and it can kill them)

innocent an innocent person does not do bad things

inspector an important policeman

judge *(n)* the most important person in a court

jury a number of people (often twelve) who listen to law cases in a court; they say that someone is innocent or not innocent

knock *(v)* to hit a door with your hand

law people write laws to tell you what is right and what is wrong

lawyer a person who knows about the law, and who helps people who do not know about the law

loudly with a lot of noise; not quietly

prison a big building for people who do something wrong (break the law); they live there and cannot leave

sell to give something to someone for money

sir a polite word when you speak to a man (e.g. *Yes, sir*)

stomach the middle part of your body in the front

sure   when you are sure about something, you know that it is true

toothpaste   you clean your teeth with toothpaste

truth   things that are true

tube   toothpaste is usually in a tube

White Death

ACTIVITIES

ACTIVITIES

Before Reading

1 Read the back cover and the story introduction on the first page of the book. How much do you know now about the story?

Tick one box for each sentence. YES NO

1 Anna Harland is Sarah's daughter. ☐ ☐

2 Sarah had heroin in her bag. ☐ ☐

3 Sarah said that it was her heroin. ☐ ☐

4 Anna thinks that it was Sarah's heroin. ☐ ☐

5 People who take heroin die. ☐ ☐

2 What is going to happen in the story? Can you guess?

Tick one box for each sentence. YES NO

1 Sarah Harland dies. ☐ ☐

2 Sarah's new boyfriend dies. ☐ ☐

3 Sarah and her new boyfriend get married. ☐ ☐

4 Sarah's old boyfriend helps her. ☐ ☐

5 Sarah goes back to England with her mother. ☐ ☐

ACTIVITIES

While Reading

Read Chapters 1 and 2.
Are these sentences true (T) or false (F)?

1 The prison is in England.
2 Sarah came to this country with Stephen.
3 Hassan is in prison too.
4 The heroin was in a box of chocolates.
5 Sarah worked in a hospital so she knew about heroin.

Read Chapter 3. Use these words from the story to complete this paragraph. (Use each word once.)

die, kills, happy, airport, tubes, money, Death, toothpaste, bags, telephoned

People take heroin because at first it makes them _____.
But in the end it _____ them. This is why it is called the
White _____. People sell heroin for lots of _____. The law
says that people who bring heroin into the country must
_____. Someone _____ the police and said that a young
man and a young woman had heroin in their _____. When
Sarah and Hassan arrived at the _____, the police looked
in their bags. They found three _____ of toothpaste. But
there was heroin in the tubes, not _____.

Read Chapter 4. Who said this? Who were they talking to? Who or what were they talking about?

1 'But Sarah – he was your boyfriend for two years!'
2 'He doesn't love me now, and I don't love him.'
3 'That's very important.'
4 'I bought it.'
5 'Why did she carry it for you?'

Read Chapters 5 and 6. Choose the correct ending for these sentences.

1 Stephen said that . . .
   a) Sarah knew about the heroin but Hassan didn't.
   b) Hassan knew about the heroin but Sarah didn't.
   c) Hassan and Sarah both knew about the heroin.
2 Stephen told Anna to come to his hotel . . .
   a) tomorrow morning.
   b) tonight.
   c) tomorrow night.
3 Sarah is sometimes ill because . . .
   a) she takes heroin.
   b) she is going to have a baby.
   c) she is frightened.
4 The father of the baby is . . .
   a) Stephen.
   b) Mr Cheng.
   c) Hassan.

5 The law says that they can't kill . . .

  a) a woman.

  b) a woman who is going to have a baby.

  c) a man and a woman who are going to have a baby.

Read Chapters 7 and 8. Here are some untrue sentences. Change them into true sentences.

1 Sarah put the heroin in the toothpaste tubes.

2 Hassan put the heroin in Sarah's bag.

3 Stephen didn't want Hassan to die.

4 Inspector Aziz married his first girlfriend.

5 Anna knew about Stephen because she takes heroin.

6 Anna was angry about Sarah and Hassan.

7 Stephen is going to go back to England.

What is going to happen after the end of the story? What do you think?

1 Sarah and Hassan get married.

2 Stephen dies.

3 Sarah becomes a doctor.

4 Stephen's mother and father are angry with Anna.

5 Sarah and Hassan go to live in England.

ACTIVITIES

After Reading

1 **Choose the odd one out in these groups of words.**

   1 police, prison, baby, arrest, inspector

   2 daughter, judge, court, jury, lawyer

   3 hospital, doctor, drug, ill, toothpaste

   4 airport, plane, heroin, bag, hotel

2 **Fill in the chart with information about the people. Then use the information to write a short description of each person. Use pronouns (*he, she*, etc.) and join your sentences with *and* where possible.**

Example: *Sarah is 19. She is tall and she . . .*

	Age	Body	Face, eyes	Job
Sarah	19	tall		
Anna				
Hassan				
Inspector Aziz				

3 **The chapters in this book do not have titles. Here is a list of titles. Choose one for each chapter.**

Sarah's story   Hassan's story

In prison   Inspector Aziz

Heroin kills   Stephen is angry

Stephen's story   Sarah is ill

4 **Here is a conversation between Anna and Inspector Aziz. It is in the wrong order. Write it out in the correct order and put in the speakers' names. Aziz speaks first (number 8).**

1 _____ 'Because his eyes are very big and dark, and his body is always moving.'

2 _____ 'Go to Stephen's hotel early tomorrow morning. Show this tube of toothpaste to him. It has heroin in it.'

3 _____ 'I think that he takes heroin.'

4 _____ 'I think that you are right. So I want you to help me.'

5 _____ 'I'm going to be outside the door. I'm going to listen to what he says.'

6 _____ 'Of course, Inspector. What can I do?'

7 _____ 'Why do you think that?'

8 *Aziz* 'You're a doctor. What do you think about Stephen, Mrs Harland?'

9 _____ 'But how can that help?'

5 **Here is a new illustration for the story. Find the best place in the story to put the picture, and answer these questions.**

The picture goes on page _____.

1 Who are the people in this picture?

2 Where are they now, and where are they going to go?

3 What is the young man going to say? Can you imagine?

Now write a caption for the picture.

Caption: _____

6 Choose answers to these questions.

1 The law in this story says that people who bring heroin into the country must die. Is this right?
   a) Yes. The law must punish people who do bad things.
   b) No. It is always wrong to kill people, and sometimes the wrong person dies.
   c) Perhaps. It is better for the judge to decide each time.

2 When Hassan hit the police car, his father bought a new car for the police and Hassan didn't go to prison. Was this right?
   a) Yes. It was just an accident. Hassan didn't kill anyone.
   b) No. People who do something bad must go to prison.
   c) Perhaps. Rich people can pay, so they don't go to prison. But what about poor people?

7 What do you think about Sarah's two boyfriends?

1 'It was my toothpaste,' Hassan said to the court. Why did he say that? Was he right to say it?

2 'Of course I love Sarah,' Stephen said to Anna. Do you think that was true? Why, or why not?

ABOUT THE AUTHOR

Tim Vicary is an experienced teacher and writer, and has written several stories for the Oxford Bookworms Library. Many of these are in the Thriller & Adventure series, such as *Chemical Secret* (at Stage 3), or in the True Stories series, such as *Mutiny on the Bounty* (at Stage 1), which tells the story of Captain Bligh and his voyage to the south seas. He has also published two long novels, *The Blood upon the Rose* and *Cat and Mouse*.

Tim Vicary has two children, and keeps dogs, cats, and horses. He lives and works in York, in the north of England.

OXFORD BOOKWORMS LIBRARY

Classics • Crime & Mystery • Factfiles • Fantasy & Horror
Human Interest • Playscripts • Thriller & Adventure
True Stories • World Stories

The OXFORD BOOKWORMS LIBRARY provides enjoyable reading in English, with a wide range of classic and modern fiction, non-fiction, and plays. It includes original and adapted texts in seven carefully graded language stages, which take learners from beginner to advanced level. An overview is given on the next pages.

All Stage 1 titles are available as audio recordings, as well as over eighty other titles from Starter to Stage 6. All Starters and many titles at Stages 1 to 4 are specially recommended for younger learners. Every Bookworm is illustrated, and Starters and Factfiles have full-colour illustrations.

The OXFORD BOOKWORMS LIBRARY also offers extensive support. Each book contains an introduction to the story, notes about the author, a glossary, and activities. Additional resources include tests and worksheets, and answers for these and for the activities in the books. There is advice on running a class library, using audio recordings, and the many ways of using Oxford Bookworms in reading programmes. Resource materials are available on the website <www.oup.com/elt/gradedreaders>.

The *Oxford Bookworms Collection* is a series for advanced learners. It consists of volumes of short stories by well-known authors, both classic and modern. Texts are not abridged or adapted in any way, but carefully selected to be accessible to the advanced student.

You can find details and a full list of titles in the *Oxford Bookworms Library Catalogue* and *Oxford English Language Teaching Catalogues*, and on the website <www.oup.com/elt/gradedreaders>.

THE OXFORD BOOKWORMS LIBRARY
GRADING AND SAMPLE EXTRACTS

STARTER • 250 HEADWORDS

present simple – present continuous – imperative –
can/cannot, must – going to (future) – simple gerunds ...

Her phone is ringing – but where is it?

Sally gets out of bed and looks in her bag. No phone. She looks under the bed. No phone. Then she looks behind the door. There is her phone. Sally picks up her phone and answers it. ***Sally's Phone***

STAGE 1 • 400 HEADWORDS

... past simple – coordination with *and, but, or* –
subordination with *before, after, when, because, so* ...

I knew him in Persia. He was a famous builder and I worked with him there. For a time I was his friend, but not for long. When he came to Paris, I came after him – I wanted to watch him. He was a very clever, very dangerous man. ***The Phantom of the Opera***

STAGE 2 • 700 HEADWORDS

... present perfect – *will* (future) – *(don't) have to, must not, could* –
comparison of adjectives – simple *if* clauses – past continuous –
tag questions – *ask/tell* + infinitive ...

While I was writing these words in my diary, I decided what to do. I must try to escape. I shall try to get down the wall outside. The window is high above the ground, but I have to try. I shall take some of the gold with me – if I escape, perhaps it will be helpful later. ***Dracula***

STAGE 3 • 1000 HEADWORDS

... should, may – present perfect continuous – *used to* – past perfect –
causative – relative clauses – indirect statements ...

Of course, it was most important that no one should see
Colin, Mary, or Dickon entering the secret garden. So Colin
gave orders to the gardeners that they must all keep away
from that part of the garden in future. *The Secret Garden*

STAGE 4 • 1400 HEADWORDS

... past perfect continuous – passive (simple forms) –
would conditional clauses – indirect questions –
relatives with *where/when* – gerunds after prepositions/phrases ...

I was glad. Now Hyde could not show his face to the world
again. If he did, every honest man in London would be proud
to report him to the police. *Dr Jekyll and Mr Hyde*

STAGE 5 • 1800 HEADWORDS

... future continuous – future perfect –
passive (modals, continuous forms) –
would have conditional clauses – modals + perfect infinitive ...

If he had spoken Estella's name, I would have hit him. I was so
angry with him, and so depressed about my future, that I could
not eat the breakfast. Instead I went straight to the old house.
Great Expectations

STAGE 6 • 2500 HEADWORDS

... passive (infinitives, gerunds) – advanced modal meanings –
clauses of concession, condition

When I stepped up to the piano, I was confident. It was as if I
knew that the prodigy side of me really did exist. And when I
started to play, I was so caught up in how lovely I looked that
I didn't worry how I would sound. *The Joy Luck Club*

BOOKWORMS · THRILLER & ADVENTURE · STAGE 1

Goodbye, Mr Hollywood

JOHN ESCOTT

Nick Lortz is sitting outside a café in Whistler, a village in the Canadian mountains, when a stranger comes and sits next to him. She's young, pretty, and has a beautiful smile. Nick is happy to sit and talk with her.

But why does she call Nick 'Mr Hollywood'? Why does she give him a big kiss when she leaves? And who is the man at the next table – the man with short white hair?

Nick learns the answer to these questions three long days later – in a police station on Vancouver Island.

BOOKWORMS · TRUE STORIES · STAGE 1

Ned Kelly: A True Story

CHRISTINE LINDOP

When he was a boy, he was poor and hungry. When he was a young man, he was still poor and still hungry. He learnt how to steal horses, he learnt how to fight, he learnt how to live – outside the law. Australia in the 1870s was a hard, wild place. Rich people had land, poor people didn't. So the rich got richer, and the poor stayed poor.

Some say Ned Kelly was a bad man. Some say he was a good man but the law was bad. This is the true story of Australia's most famous outlaw.